Happy Day® Coloring Book

Who Made BABY ANIMALS?

illustrated by Norma Garris

The Standard Publishing Company, Cincinnati, Ohio. A division of Standex International Corporation.
 ISBN 0-7847-0436-8. Designed by Coleen Davis.

Who made the fawn?

Who made the kitten?

Who made the calf?

Who made the birds?

Who made the lamb?

Who made the squirrel?

Who made the chick?

Who made the duckling?

Who made the colt?

Who made the puppy?

God made us all!

Genesis 1